I

AMERICAN BOOK SERIES AWARDS

Sponsored By:

SAN DIEGO POETS PRESS
Editor/Publisher: Kathleen Iddings

The Counting of Grains	by	Joan LaBombard	*1989*
Yarrow Field	by	Regina McBride	*1990*
The Only Cure I Know	by	Charles Atkinson	*1991*
Hometown, USA	by	Michael Cleary	*1992*
Someone Had To Live	by	Kevin Griffith	*1993*

San Diego Poets Press is a not-for-profit organization originated in 1981 for the purpose of supporting contemporary poetry and poets, and furthering the literary arts in general. We gratefully acknowledge those who have supported our efforts:

California Arts Council

Security Pacific Bank

Danah Fayman

Union Bank

Finch, Pruyn & Company, Inc.

In Memory of Edith Brooks Herman

Anonymous Donors

San Diego Poets Press
Editor/Publisher: Kathleen Iddings
P.O. Box 8638
La Jolla, CA 92038

IV

SOMEONE
HAD TO LIVE

Poems by Kevin Griffith

San Diego Poets Press
La Jolla

Copyright: Kevin Griffith, 1994
ISBN: 0-931289-14-9
Library of Congress Catalog Number: 93-061679

Cover Design: Patricia R. Barnett
PRB•ASSOCIATES
127 Spinnaker Court
Del Mar, CA 92014

SAN DIEGO POETS PRESS
P.O. Box 8638
La Jolla, CA 92038
Kathleen Iddings, Editor/Publisher

Grateful acknowledgment is made to the following magazines in which these poems first appeared, sometimes in different form:

College English: "North of Bridgeport: Morel Hunting."

The Cream City Review: "Miner" (printed as "Labor").

Mid-American Review: "While Watching My Father…"

The Minnesota Review: "The Pond Near Crematorium Four."

National Forum: "Shooting Bottles."

New York Quarterly: "Storm Guard #1005…"

Permafrost: "Stillbirth," "Songs of the Fisherwoman," "The Last Days of Edward Manigault," and "Manigault in Downpour."

The Plum Review: "Evening Storm, Round Lake."

Poesie Europe (Frankfurt): "Three Songs for a Woman."

Poet & Critic: "Rain, Light, Architecture."

Poet Lore: "In the Middle of Nowhere."

The Quarterly: "Shoes," "The Canal," "The Water Gatherer," and "The Loss Trader."

The Southern Review: "Reef Boy."

Yankee: "Good" and "These Days."

The Wallace Stevens Journal: "Heaven"

A number of these poems also appeared in *Labors*, a chapbook published by Stillwaters Press, and *Manigault's Hunger*, a chapbook published by *Permafrost* (University of Alaska Fairbanks Press).

Contents

I Your Reflection Walks Out of You

The Fisherwoman   15
Three Songs for a Woman   17
Stillbirth   18
The Vase   19
These Days   20
Good   21

II The Last Days of Edward Manigault

Etching   25
Paint by Number   26
Manigault in Downpour   28
The Last Days of Edward Manigault   29
The Loss Trader   36

III The Coffin Nailed with Clouds

Evening Storm, Round Lake   41
Soapberries   42
Watching My Father Work on his Car,
    I Fall Asleep in my Lawn Chair   43
Whiskey   44
Shooting Bottles   45
In an Old Man's House   46
Heaven   47
The Canal   48

IV Intercessions

The Pond Near Crematorium Four   53
Rain, Light, Architecture   54
North of Bridgeport: Morel Hunting   55
In the Middle of Nowhere   56
After the Bombing, Another President's
    Approval Rating Rises   57
Atlantic City, Scattered Showers   58
Notes from the Strangler   59
Miner   61
Shoes   62
Water Gatherer   63
Storm Guard #1005 Receives Orders to Liquidate
    Corpses and Destroy Evidence   64
Reef Boy   65
Grandfathers   66

For My Parents

I

Your Reflection Walks Out of You

The Fisherwoman

i

I remember my first son,
the one that came blue and looking old.
I placed the body in a cradle
between two willow roots so large
they had burst through the earth
the way the backs of carp
break a river's surface.
I wish his father had stayed to bury him.

ii

Today is measured by sheephead:
one before noon, a bite later.
By nightfall I have two.
Their bodies move in the bucket slowly,
dull silver, but alive,
a borrowed beauty,
the way the moon borrows the sun.

iii

I have no boat. I place my chair
on the pier and let waves
sail to me. This land is its own giant raft
moving slowly through the water.

iv

Fishing is a ceremony for the dead.
Of all the things fishing is compared to,

no one mentions judgment.
Your reflection walks out of you
and floats on its back only so long.
Everything you catch, even the most bloated catfish,
must tear through your likeness.

v

People on the boats know me as Mary.
I don't think I'll ever take a husband.
The people float by saying "Mary," "Mary."
I can't help but wonder if names are cruel.

vi

In the end I know I'll ask if it was all worth it.
I'll turn my back, my reflection rolling face down
in the water. So many days and so many fish.
If God is kind, you'll see an empty chair,
an empty bucket, and a pole. Throw them in.
The raft is yours to keep.

Three Songs for a Woman

Your body is thin
like a thread, strong
the way a thread
is made of still smaller threads.

When you walk, you move
quietly, like a child's story—
the last pages of your steps
turning into sleep.

Your words are not even,
but angled, the way
a candle is cut
so that its purpose is not
to last, but to melt,
to make bottles beautiful.

Stillbirth

You cradled the body delicately,
like a bunch of August flowers.
You spoke to it quietly,
as if the dead could understand a murmur.

Sometimes happiness fills a belly. So delicately
you run your hands over the pale flowers
of your skin. But sorrow can work quietly,
arriving in light without a murmur.

Now you rest in bed for days, your head delicately
propped against the pillow. The flowers
of your silence have bloomed quietly
into a meadow. The fan murmurs

in the open window, delicately
bending the tall grasses and flowers
that keep distance between two people. Quietly
I move from your room, the murmur

of a conversation, a few words, delicately
fading in my head. The white flowers
of stars fall into place. Quietly.
Not even a murmur.

The Vase

You stare at the ceiling, your
mouth open like a hungry bird's.

Because your are more
than bottle, you must thirst
for the light, so that when we look close,
we see the tiny rivers
of glass, the little planets of air.

You live a sad life. At most
you are a house for the dying
and the dead: your voice of dried
petals, your body filled with old water.

These Days

These days, caught between the taste
of wind and the lacy remnants of smoke,

a leaf drops with the weight of thought.
To understand how the present grows around us,

you have to stand on a bridge, so that below
there is a small island dense with grass

no one cares to cut. And you must know
that geese are not always in the sky

but rustling among the girders, their sounds
of flight in every step forward.

Days like these, you understand how the river divides
under all of us, how eddies swirl into faces,

how the white stacks of the chocolate factory
hold ghosts so sweet you wish there were ghosts.

These days, the wings are what matter. For once,
you rise and watch yourself fallen:

a solitary walker, a clipped angel.

Good

Good, my son asked, what
is *good*?

Good, I said, look
in your hands—
when you need it
there's a pale cup,
cracked a bit, I know.

Speak into it,
and it fills with the soft liquid
of your voice.

II

The Last Days of Edward Manigault

The artist Manigault died while fasting in an attempt to hallucinate more vivid colors.

Etching

In the land where the bones live
the skeletons are held together
by ink, the way the walls of a storm
are stitched together by lightning.

The ancient people believe that a
face drawn in anger makes
the maker's prayers rise higher,
makes the words uttered in silence

ride horses to the next world.
That is the power of a hand
and a piece of ash. The soft wood
we burn for our salvation
traces over the sad rags of paper.
We hold that ash in our hands.
We draw our lives with what we hold.

Paint by Number

One.
White, the no color,
the beginning of everything,
the blink of an eye
turned on its side.

Zero.
Clear, a nothing, as transparent
as a peek-hole.
Yet it is this emptiness
that gives the door its eye.
You live as its mind,
watching each visitor.

But zero is also the silent cry.
You fall into zero like an old well.
You fall forever, waiting
for the bitter water, the rust.

Five.
Five has to be red.
It is an angry number—every price has a five.
Two fives equal ten,
and when you have lost ten,
you have been decimated.

Eight.
Black is infinity. Infinity at its most human,
standing straight up
like a sentry. Yet it doesn't need
to watch us too carefully.
We can never sneak up on eight.
It always walks just far enough ahead of us.

Six.
Calm, blue, a soft round number,
shaped like a tear.
Type a row of sixes
and you will see the page cry.

Four.
Yellow, never humble,
persistent as a wild flower,
as a child's *why?*

Seven.
And seven, seven is tricky,
the number of luck and death,
the both/and number, color of old dice,
the gray.

Manigault in Downpour

Olive, the color of a bad bruise, feathers
into a corner of sky, seeps in, like rain
in a faulty coffin, when we know the dead cry
long after the sorrows of the living are over.

I look at the flower clipped to my pocket,
its purple folds wadded like crepe paper,
some relic of an old party.
In a grand hall laughter grows like a carnation.

Using the small stair of its body, ivy climbs
my mistress's window. I see her face through
the iron cross in the pane, crow-blue,
and then the face of another beside her.
My heart sinks like the fish in the pond,
and I know the green lace which is their sky.

A newspaper clings to the mailbox,
words disintegrating like the ghost of a chance.
I am glad S is such a sad letter, the beautiful curve
of the sleeper's body, the beautiful waltz
of the sleep walker.

All at once, my umbrella falls from my hand
and lands upside down on the sidewalk.
It hurries away on its sharp metal foot,
its steps sounding very much like the persistence of rain.

The Last Days of Edward Manigault

November 3, 1910

Outside, the sky grays like an old saint.
Rain is seasoned with soot. New York.

I've been reading of the shamans, how they journey
living on nothing but prayer, until their eyes
are pierced by the arrow of spirits,
that wound which lets in a different light,
God's light. On my plate, some scallions
and a square of brown bread.
I wash it down with tea. My last swallow.

November 4

An empty plate of moon.
A white canvas. Evening.

My work progresses in fits and starts.
A color leaves my brush for canvas
and ceases to have relevance.
It dies like a wave: the beauty
is in the crashing, the stroke on cloth.
What's left is merely foam and sand.
In frustration, I paint the canvas black,
closing its eye, sending it to sleep.

In my dreams, I walk across a desert
carrying a walking stick made of hair.
Dune after dune I travel, the stick
becoming heavier as I realize I cannot
capture even the color of sand,
color of monotony. In the distance, a great canyon,
a bowl scooped into rock, mottled
with the colors of snake leather. I am a visitor
in one of my own landscapes, traveling toward
an artificial horizon. No matter how long I walk,
I am already as far as I have been
and as far as I will go.

November 7

A bubble sealed in amber.
My studio.

The jars of oil paint rest on a table: burnt umber
swirled with turquoise and jade, violet with cream
and parrot. Some colors have not mixed well
and remain in perpetual swirling, like the galaxy
of milk that forms in coffee
when white slips into brown.

Someone enters without a knock.
I cannot see past the candle tongue.
The shadow speaks with a woman's voice:
I have brought you food.
Are you a nurse?
I take care of men. I live here. I have seen you.
What do I look like?
Like a man who wants to die. I've seen many like you.
If I eat, I will not see.
A strange thought.
Do you know all the names for yellow?
Here is half a loaf and cheese.
Canary, lemon, jasmine, saffron....

The shadow is gone. I return to work,
wondering if there is a true color for rain.

November 9

The stars continue their slow somnambulant waltz.

I rest on my cot, reminded of the story of an amnesiac
who awoke one day remembering
nothing of his own life but speaking another language.
I think of the genius left to be opened,
the brain's little vaults.

In my dream, I am walking down a gray hallway:
my hand touches an iron door. The lock is rusted
and crumbles in my hand. Inside this windowless room
are all the colors I can imagine, yet as I reach for them,
they become fruit, bread, meat. A stern-looking man
gathers the food onto a plate and eats them
while I am forced to watch.

I wake, feeling as if I have painted all night.
My mind is weary and the canvas is black.

November 12

Sky a grayish violet.
Cloud a Lagerfeld rose.

Sound of a bell, a distant bell, like the faraway echo
one hears inside his own hollow body.
I must drink a small glass of water
to keep my mouth moist. The water is a gypsy;
borrowing its color the way the ocean's green
is really the alchemy of murk,
sea flower, and sky.

I look through the bottom of my glass
to the bare wood floor; all the various grains
ripple and contort. I am standing on a silt carpet,
waiting for the prophets, the messengers of color.
But they are spies, draped in velvet cloaks,
and in the corners of my vision,
I can sense them following.
When I turn to face them, they disappear.

November 15

Blue hair of mold.
Dried cheese.

The shadow again.

You have not eaten?
Even black has its nuances.
I will bring a doctor, if I can find one for the poor.
May I see your eyes?
My eyes? You must eat.
What color is worry that swims behind eyes like a shark?
You cannot live on your colors.
Ebony, jet, sable, ink...

The shadow disappears.

I remember my mistress, the wife of a printer.
O, the blackness of her letters, the dark words shadowing
the curl of her body as she slept.
Black and white are simple, clean. The colors of accounts.
I stare into my black canvas. In its impasto terrain
live thousands of tiny skeletons.

November 17

Fireworks.
I have decided to paint fireworks. The grand kind,
like I witnessed as a child along the Hudson River.
For that is what I now see—pinpoints of light—not the stars
that flourish when one stands too quickly, but a steady net
of light speckled over my face. A veil of light.
God is sharing his colors for joy and sadness,
giving me a veil, something one wears as a bride or a mourner.

A color between jade and pink
blossoms in my mind, sending tendrils
up the crisscross of light in front of my face.
My brush becomes a tiny oar. I am ready to make a great journey.
The tip of my brush ripples into blackness.

The Loss Trader

He was a man whose trade
was loss. At 12, he buried
a tin soldier and a Mercury dime
in the peach grove near his home,
thinking that, at some
great distance in his life,
they would come back to him.

In his old neighborhood,
roofs were covered
with toy rockets. Tiny gray boats
littered the river. The wind combed
its hair with balsa and paper.

Now, as he sleeps, chessmen are retreating
under the sofa. His wife's pale body rolls
and sinks beneath waves
of blanket. In some orchard that grows
in his dream, a poor soldier savors
fallen fruit. He is preparing
for the long march home.

III

The Coffin Nailed With Clouds

Evening Storm, Round Lake

Along the water, roots
hold tight to souls.
I've stood at this shore
many times, quiet as a statue
waking from its dream of hands.

Thunder rumbles as if clouds
are carrying cargoes of sound.
No one on the far shore. Evening
spreads through the water,
lights catching the shallows,
like the movements of fish
close to the surface.

I remember my father kept a stone
in his tackle box, found
while digging graves.
He had no reason for keeping it,
except that it was good and round,
good because he had dug the way
for someone else.

What is it that I have to keep?
In the bottom of my glass,
a dried flower of wine.

I find my shadow darkening
like an anchor. The more I move,
the more the water closes in.
Nothing—stone nor wine—
can do my wanting for me.

Soapberries

My father counts them out,
hands them to me carefully:
three for me, three for you,
the precious fruit, the pale bowl;
they sagged in their syrup
like tired eyes.

I remember how they tasted
so far away and ancient,
like the smell of walls
and plaster on his hands.
Looking into the bowl,
I still hear his story —
the one about the coffin maker
in heaven, who nails the lids
with clouds.

Watching My Father Work on His Car, I Fell Asleep in My Lawn Chair

The book falls from my hand, face down,
and makes a little tent on the ground.

What wants to be free of me
is leaving, my arms sliding
like white eels through the weeds,
my feet following one another
across the avenues of the grass.

My father bows
in the whirring cage of engine.

The sun drains back through the leaves
I crawl into the shelter of my words.
A yellow light blinks from my father's hands.

Whiskey

Let us drink which has nothing to tell you
open its umbrella over your sorrows.
Let the comfort of its quiet voice
dance with the shadow of your doubt.

And let the square bottle, let its fluted neck
bow to you once more.
Let the others labor in the field,
let others sweat among the ragweed.

Listen, let this liquid copper be
a currency. If the moon were a coin,
we'd all be poor, one thin dime. But with you,
Mr. Daniels, Sir Daniels, we are big spenders

indeed, a little tip here, a big tip for the real pros.
Let the book remain open, like a face
which paints itself with guilt. Let the light
work up through the bottom of the glass.

Let us see ourselves as we really are.
Let us listen to the branches click in the wind,
click, click—the last sounds a man hears
who pleads for his life.

Shooting Bottles

Behind the toppled chicken coop,
in the old burn pit, the rain
makes a sea. Glass ships
are sinking: wine bottles, brown jugs,
the square whiskey flask

leaving its blue slick, shapeless
as a drunkdard's words. The glass
is getting all the rounds I have,
taking back the water that lifted it
for the hunter, my need to shoot.

I sit all day on the fallen walnut's trunk,
listening to the rain, to the crack of emptiness
growing webs then sinking.
I remember when my father showed me
the bullet scars on his chest and back,

after he left the hospital.
"You don't know what it's like
to wake up and see nothing."
When silence returns, it is soft and welcoming
as the grassy place where deer sleep.

In an Old Man's House

He remembers his days of dark hair and tobacco.
The last good drink he's had: Dallas,
1973, double Johnny, no rocks.

Every so often history answers with a kiss.
He remembers Jenny, Matilda, the ivory
inside of an arm, the flowers of breath,

the perfectly cruel little things they all said.

Hip gone, he doesn't get much sweat—
life is clipped on a laundry line every week
or so. And he always remembers the small bits,

the socks, the underwear, but the pants,
the pants take longer, they stay in the rain.
So he sits in his white shower chair,

thinking of the lemons, how they grow
on the tree out back without him, without
his careful hands, his shears.

His one good tree.

At night, he hears the wind talking.
It can't die either. It tosses and turns
like a man who dreams of work.

Heaven

Heaven means precisely: the impossibility
of crows. Heaven means the warm snow
of a father's last word. Heaven means

the vault where all green things are stored
remains open, endures, yet each of us has
a key for that June place regardless.

Heaven means the memory of rain. It means
the thought of sleep, and when you wake
in your gray mind's bed, you're only dreaming.

Heaven is like that. Heaven is the tongue's
dead weight. The last need of speaking passed
along with the spare change of blind eyes;

your last thought took flight and sits on a line,
like an impossible crow. Heaven can be
funny that way. Heaven likes to joke.

The smile of heaven says *forever*,
and it means it, like a proud father naming
a child before it's born. We look into the light,

and we have a name. And we live and we die.

The Canal

Remembering is an old canal:
what used to connect
is now full of humidity and darkness,
its granite walls mortared
with lichen and moss.

I remember how we crossed
a long wooden bridge.
Upstream, the state had planted
steel girders to stop trees and debris
from toppling the bridge.
The girders grew proud
with rust and wreckage.

Father,
when I finally reached the water,
I stood on the stone landing and listened
to fish break the surface.
You told me they would feed on anything,
even stones and seeds, if that's all you had.
I kicked in some dust,
and watched a school of shadows move in.

IV

Intercessions

The Pond Near Crematorium Four

The remains of as many as 4,416 prisoners
were dumped into the pond daily.

When the wasp landed
on my hand, I was not surprised.
Of course, in summer
the fruit ripens, bursts, and falls
for the hunger of insects.
I saw it for a fraction
before it left its small signature of pain
and could only clench
and squint away the hurt.

Now, our guide's red dress flaps
as she leads us through
cautioning fields, each long blade
wind bent. She stops, slips
her arm in pond's shallows,
and lifts the bone chips
into my hand,
light and delicate as wasps.

Rain, Light, Architecture

At night, workers leave a few lights
burning at the construction area. They glow
with a far-off sadness, the way
a single bulb clings to life
in a corner of a cellar, or the way
a few lights remain shining underwater
as a ship goes down. In this different light,
you also see rain in many ways:
each drop a leaden globe, a bit of solder,
or melded together, as if rain were building
walls, forging itself with girders,
climbing down the ladders.
All night the water follows a reckless plan.
You arrive at a new office. A key drips from your hand.

North of Bridgeport: Morel Hunting

The sky's soft light—white, with a signature of darkness,
like birch or the quiet beginning of storm. In gullies,

I look for the gray and furrowed, the little brains
growing in stump shadow, remember their sweet taste

with butter and flour. Down the ravine, blue wreck
of a child's wading pool, walls buckled

and torn as the mills along the Ohio, windows coated
with soot, black as the insides of oven doors.

I think of the workers, their voices of mill smoke.
To sleep on iron pillows with iron wives.

Up ahead, the graveyard, the scattered sunflowers
growing among the stones—

so many black faces turning in the wind
as if they sense they are being followed.

Around here, even if your bag stays empty,
Ohio won't let you go empty-handed.
You carry your delicacies. You pay for them.

In the Middle of Nowhere

Across the nights, stars shower
like sparks off a grindstone.
Here, the blade of forever
has left the bramble to grow,
to finger its sawtooth thorns
up the latticework of your life.
In the tangle, you are more
than lost: the less you try,
the closer you are to home.
And you spend your days
gathering what your torn
hands can find, the stray
berries staining your mouth.
This is nowhere. You live on that truth.

After the Bombing, Another President's Approval Rating Rises

How we like the falling away, the sudden
weight-loss of rockets, the sweepstake rush
and sway over the landscape, the silvery
glide of the winged fish, eyeless,
blind with one thought on the map
in its mind.

Oh sure, the killing is easy.
Anyone can tell you that.
And in the time it takes you to read this,
3,000 people will die of...
but we all know that too.
The numbers skip harmlessly in our minds
filling the spaces between our thoughts
like the words of an empty song.

The sad weight of our lives has collapsed
into itself, dense as an old star.
Crowds move so close these days.
They swallow us whole.
We walk quietly into those places
where no light returns.

Atlantic City, Scattered Showers

Tonight, even the weather can't get it right.
The thunder dreams, snoring like a prize fighter,

stirring only slightly at times, mumbling
recollections of days when it had ambition,

when a storm was a *storm*, the real show,
a drumming so loud it put bruises

on the faces of neighborhoods. Around here
it's hard to tell storm from man, the punch drunk,

those who walk like devils of wind, swirling
briefly with the good hands, then dying in a broomful

of ash. It's a long walk indeed, one plank
to the next, enough wood for a village's worth

of caskets, but you take it—you must;
you live a life and this is it,

your palms rubbed gray with the faces
of coins, your shoes wired shut,

the weight of a stolen ashtray
wearing through the cloth of your pocket.

Notes from the Strangler

I.

You do not know what it is
to gaze in the tiny rivers
of your palms, to read
the nail scars on the back
of your two strong hands,
scars vaguely red and scattered
like lips, the remnants
of a hundred soft kisses.

II.

I miss my sleep.
I miss that fine line separating
one world from the next,
like a wall a cold current
that wavers near the deep parts
of a deep lake, the wall that keeps
the small fish away, that place
where light drowns as if
it were tied with rope
and weighted with stone.

III.

The last dream I had was a good one.
I remember it well.
I was a man walking to my job
like any other man.
My wallet weighed heavy
in my coat pocket,
rocking against my chest
as I stepped,
like a second heart.

IV.

My mother sang to me
in the cradle. I remember
how her songs fell from
her lips and floated above
my hands. The words seemed
to hang from strings like
a baby's toy, just out of reach.
How I tried and tried to grab them,
my hands groping in the air.

V.

If you find these, I'll be dead.
Or maybe alive. Right now
my hands are the only way
to keep things straight:
night and day,
asleep and awake,
you or me.

Miner

I know no other work.
I place my pick against
the anthracite, chipping
away crumbs of fuel.

What good does it do?

I remember a story of a baker
who built his house
out of bricks of bread.
Eventually it disappeared into birds.

Shoes

*Know that from this day forth
Shoes shall be called coffins.*
     —Nicanor Parra

Take note: you are walking
to your grave.

You will notice at the shore
the many little coffins
tossed in the sand
while the dead wade for hours,

and in the evening how exquisitely
coffins glide across
the ballroom. How polished they are,
reflecting the chandeliers.

You will notice the trail of coffins
across new snow, the open coffins
beside the bed, the poem resting
in the coffins of its strict rhythm.

Many sunny days you will see
more dead than ever. They walk
hand in hand under the elms,
wearing their future: eyes, tongue, sole, lace.

The Water Gatherer

Sometimes my prayers go unanswered.
But if smoke always listened,
why would I pray?

I walk many miles over sand,
riding my shadow like the snake.
During proper visions

I stop to make offerings,
but my medicine bag grows thin
like a sin that is forgotten.

A spider does not
need bones. The lake woman
does not need my ashes.

Somewhere in the invisible water
she laughs. She will sleep,
hiding under her mirror,
knowing I cannot steal her blood.

After the eighteenth sun,
my spirit climbs the dead tree;
the branches are arrows
shot end-to-end,
making a ladder to the sky.

Storm Guard #1005 Receives Orders to Liquidate Corpses and Destroy Evidence

My orders:

Unearth all remaining bodies. *This will be easy.*
The soil is so thin, like dust gathered
on the pages of an opened book.
There will be no need for shovels.
We must use the hooks.

Burn them using the procedure. *This will not be difficult.*
The few live ones will work the ovens, as usual.
We keep them drunk, until they too are liquidated.
Except we have no wine.

Crush any remaining bones to dust. *There will not be time.*
We must mix the fragments with gravel.
The road that led them in will lead them out.
That's the best we can do.

Destroy the compound and seed the area. *They will know.*
They will walk on the dead, they will drink the dead from ponds,
they will breathe hair and ashes settling in the wind.
You cannot hide memory under a chaos of weeds.

Reef Boy

Sulu Islands, The Philippines

The fisherman slips a thin rope
around my neck, sixty feet,
ties at the other end
a heavy iron bell.
This is the scare line.

I swim with a row
of other boys. We splash,
bob our necks, drag
the bells like anchors
over the hard coral, ring
out a sound
deep as distant churches.

A school darts toward the net.
Imagine a tree swaying
in a good summer wind, leaves
full of motion—
except the leaves are flesh,
the tree, invisible,
the wind, fear.

Sometimes when the fishermen
are hauling in, the net
tangles on the rough coral, and I
have to dive to free it.
When my breath is gone
and the net still isn't free,
I look up at the surface,
like heaven, so many black shadows
swimming in a blue sky.

Grandfathers

Life was hard. Every night, a sandbag for a pillow.
They took us to the stadium and counted us out.

For two weeks I waded in trench mud up to my knees.
For six days I rode a train, digging for air with a spoon.

I ate biscuits soaked with rain and tin.
I saw people take bread from a dead man's hand.

When the bombs hit, God grew overnight, like a vine.
God wore my father's face, the last time I saw him.

I kept a page of the Bible stitched in my sleeve.
He always told me, "God is infinite in his wisdom."

They told us to wear masks and everything would be all right.
They told us it would kill lice, and they wore the masks.

When the yellow fog soaked into my chest,
my first thought was my young wife.

I knew it was over from the start. But when they
pulled my body out, my wife was hidden safe.

One thing is true: Someone will live. Someone will live.